MAKE MONEY WITH AI

Your Guide to Unlocking Profits in the Age of Artificial Intelligence

Hassan Kalakesh

Table of content :

2. Communication and collaboration

3. Problem-solving

IV. Monetizing AI Projects:

A. Creating AI-based products:

1. Developing software applications

2. Building AI-powered tools

B. Offering AI services:

1. Consultation and advisory services

2. Customized solutions for businesses

C. Exploring AI in entrepreneurship:

1. Startups and innovation

2. Partnership opportunities

V. Chat GPT: A Specialized Section:

A. Introduction to Chat GPT:

1. Overview of conversational AI

2. Potential applications

B. Leveraging Chat GPT for Monetization:

1. Content creation and blogging

2. Virtual assistance and customer support

3. Social media management

C. Case Studies:

1. Success stories of individuals/companies using Chat GPT

2. Lessons learned and best practices.

VI. Legal and Ethical Considerations:

A. Intellectual property and data privacy

B. Ethical considerations in AI monetization

C. Compliance with regulations and standards

VII. Future Trends in AI Monetization:

A. Emerging technologies in AI:

1. Generative AI advancements

2. AI in decentralized finance

B. Predictions and forecasts for the AI market

VIII. Conclusion:

A. Recap of key points

B. Encouragement and motivation for readers

C. Call-to-action for embarking on AI monetization journey

IX. Additional Resources:

A. Recommended books, courses, and websites for further learning

B. Tools and platforms for AI development and deployment.

Introduction

The 21st century has witnessed an unprecedented surge in technological advancements, and at the forefront of this revolution is Artificial Intelligence (AI). The AI landscape has evolved from theoretical concepts to tangible applications that permeate various industries, transforming the way we live and work. As we stand on the cusp of an AI-driven future, there lies a vast and untapped opportunity for individuals and businesses to not only harness the power of AI but also to monetize it effectively.

A. Overview of the AI Landscape

Artificial Intelligence encompasses a diverse array of technologies that enable machines to simulate human intelligence. This includes Machine Learning, Natural Language Processing, Computer Vision, and more. Machine Learning, in particular, has emerged as a game-changer, allowing systems to learn from data and improve their performance without explicit programming. Natural Language Processing empowers machines to understand and interpret human language, opening up possibilities for advanced communication between humans and machines. Computer Vision, on the other hand, enables machines to interpret and make decisions based on visual data.

The widespread adoption of AI technologies is evident across various sectors. In healthcare, AI is aiding in diagnostics and personalized treatment plans. In finance, it is optimizing risk management and fraud detection. E-commerce platforms are leveraging AI for personalized recommendations, and educational institutions are incorporating AI for personalized learning experiences. The AI landscape is dynamic, with constant innovations reshaping the way we approach and solve complex problems.

B. The Potential for Making Money with AI

The integration of AI into different industries has not only enhanced efficiency but has also created lucrative opportunities for those who understand how to harness its power. The potential for making money with AI is vast and multifaceted.

1. **AI-Based Products:** Entrepreneurs can create AI-powered products ranging from software applications to specialized tools. These products can address industry-specific challenges, automate processes, and provide innovative solutions that cater to the evolving needs of businesses and consumers.

2. **AI Services:** Offering AI services, such as consultation and customized solutions, presents another avenue for monetization. Businesses are increasingly seeking expertise to integrate AI into their operations, creating a demand for knowledgeable professionals and service providers.

3. **Entrepreneurship:** Startups are thriving in the AI space, capitalizing on innovative ideas and solutions. The potential for entrepreneurship in AI extends beyond creating standalone products to forging partnerships and collaborations that drive innovation and growth.

C. Purpose and Scope of the Book

The purpose of this book is to serve as a comprehensive guide for individuals keen on navigating the intricate landscape of AI and transforming their understanding into tangible financial success. It aims to demystify the complexities of AI, providing readers with insights into not only the technical aspects but also the practical applications that lead to monetary gains.

The scope of this book encompasses a wide range of topics, starting from understanding the diverse applications of AI across industries to building the necessary skills for effective AI implementation. It delves into the intricacies of creating AI-based products and services, exploring entrepreneurship opportunities in the AI sector. Additionally, the book provides a specialized section on leveraging Chat GPT, a powerful tool in the realm of conversational AI, for financial gains.

Through real-world examples, case studies, and practical advice, this book aims to empower readers to navigate the dynamic AI landscape with confidence. Legal and ethical considerations are also addressed, ensuring that readers are equipped to navigate the complexities of AI monetization responsibly and sustainably.

As we embark on this journey through the realms of AI and wealth creation, it is essential to recognize that the fusion of innovation and entrepreneurship in the AI space holds the key to unlocking unprecedented opportunities. This book is a roadmap for those eager to embrace the transformative power of AI and turn it into a source of enduring financial success.

II. Understanding AI Opportunities

In the dynamic landscape of Artificial Intelligence (AI), opportunities abound for those who grasp the multitude of applications and industries where AI can make a significant impact. This section aims to unravel the diverse opportunities within the AI spectrum, guiding readers through key applications and industries ripe for AI integration.

A. Exploring Various AI Applications

1. **Machine Learning and Predictive Analytics:** Machine Learning (ML) is the driving force behind AI's ability to learn and adapt. It is a powerful tool for predictive analytics, enabling systems to analyse vast datasets and make informed predictions. Whether it's predicting customer behaviour, stock market trends, or equipment failures, ML is the backbone of applications that foresee future outcomes.

2. **Natural Language Processing:** Natural Language Processing (NLP) empowers machines to understand, interpret, and generate human language. This application has revolutionized communication between humans and machines, giving rise to virtual assistants, language translation services, and sentiment analysis tools. NLP's potential extends to content creation, chatbots, and enhancing customer experiences.

3. **Computer Vision:** Computer Vision allows machines to interpret and make decisions based on visual data. This application has far-reaching implications, from facial recognition and object detection to autonomous vehicles and medical image analysis. Industries such as manufacturing, healthcare, and surveillance benefit significantly from the capabilities of Computer Vision.

B. Identifying Industries with AI Potential

1. **Healthcare:** AI is reshaping the healthcare landscape by streamlining processes, improving diagnostics, and personalizing treatment plans. Predictive analytics assist in identifying potential health risks, while image recognition tools aid in the interpretation of medical images. Virtual health assistants powered by NLP enhance patient engagement and support.

2. **Finance:** The finance industry has embraced AI for risk management, fraud detection, and algorithmic trading. Machine Learning algorithms analyse financial data, providing insights into market trends and making rapid decisions. Chatbots equipped with NLP enhance customer interactions in banking, offering personalized financial advice and support.

3. **E-commerce:** AI plays a pivotal role in e-commerce through personalized recommendations, inventory management, and fraud detection. Machine Learning algorithms analyse user behaviour to suggest products, while Computer Vision facilitates image recognition for improved search functionality. Chatbots enhance customer service by providing instant responses and personalized assistance.

4. **Education:** AI is transforming education through personalized learning experiences, adaptive learning platforms, and intelligent tutoring systems. Machine Learning algorithms analyse student performance data to tailor educational content, while NLP supports language learning applications. Virtual tutors and chatbots contribute to individualized support for students.

5. **Entertainment:** The entertainment industry leverages AI for content recommendation, content creation, and immersive experiences. Machine Learning algorithms analyse user preferences to recommend movies,

music, and games. AI-driven animation and virtual reality applications enhance creativity and audience engagement.

Understanding the vast array of AI applications and the industries where they can make a significant impact is crucial for individuals and businesses seeking to capitalize on AI opportunities. In the subsequent sections of this book, we will delve deeper into how these opportunities can be translated into tangible financial gains.

III. Building AI Skills

As the demand for AI expertise continues to soar, individuals aspiring to capitalize on the opportunities presented by Artificial Intelligence must equip themselves with a robust skill set. This section delves into the essential technical and non-technical skills necessary for navigating the intricate world of AI, ensuring that enthusiasts are well-prepared to contribute meaningfully to this transformative field.

A. Necessary Technical Skills

1. **Programming Languages (Python, R, etc.):** Proficiency in programming languages is the cornerstone of AI development. Python stands out as a dominant language due to its versatility and a rich ecosystem of libraries like TensorFlow and PyTorch for Machine Learning, and NLTK for Natural Language Processing. R is another language commonly used in statistical modeling and data analysis. A solid understanding of these languages empowers individuals to write, deploy, and optimize AI algorithms effectively.

2. **Data Analysis and Interpretation:** The ability to extract meaningful insights from data is fundamental to AI. Data analysis involves cleaning, processing, and transforming raw data into a format suitable for model training. Interpretation skills allow practitioners to draw actionable conclusions from complex datasets. Proficiency in tools like Pandas and NumPy is crucial for efficient data manipulation and analysis.

3. **Model Development and Training:** Developing and training AI models requires a deep understanding of Machine Learning algorithms. This includes selecting the appropriate model architecture, optimizing hyperparameters, and evaluating model performance. Tools like scikit-learn and Keras facilitate the

implementation of various Machine Learning models, while familiarity with deep learning frameworks like TensorFlow and PyTorch is essential for complex neural network architectures.

B. Non-Technical Skills

1. **Business Acumen:** Beyond technical expertise, a keen understanding of business concepts is essential for effectively applying AI in real-world scenarios. Individuals must be able to align AI initiatives with organizational goals, identify areas for AI implementation that provide tangible business value, and make strategic decisions that drive positive outcomes. Business acumen ensures that AI solutions are not only technically sound but also contribute meaningfully to the overall success of a project or business.

2. **Communication and Collaboration:** AI professionals often work in interdisciplinary teams, collaborating with individuals from diverse backgrounds. Effective communication skills are crucial for conveying complex technical concepts to non-technical stakeholders, fostering collaboration, and ensuring that AI solutions align with organizational objectives. The ability to articulate the value of AI in a clear and understandable manner is key to gaining support and buy-in from various stakeholders.

3. **Problem-Solving:** AI practitioners are frequently tasked with solving complex problems, from optimizing business processes to developing innovative solutions. Strong problem-solving skills involve the ability to break down intricate issues, identify key challenges, and devise effective strategies for resolution. A proactive and analytical approach to problem-solving ensures that AI projects address real-world challenges and deliver

tangible outcomes.

Building a comprehensive skill set that encompasses both technical and non-technical competencies is integral to thriving in the AI landscape. The synergy of programming proficiency, data analysis acumen, and a strategic understanding of business dynamics positions individuals as valuable contributors to the AI revolution. In the subsequent chapters, we will explore how these skills can be applied to create and monetize AI solutions effectively.

IV. Monetizing AI Projects

As the influence of Artificial Intelligence (AI) continues to permeate various industries, the opportunities for monetization are expanding at an unprecedented pace. This section elucidates the diverse avenues through which individuals and businesses can turn their AI endeavours into profitable ventures, exploring both product development and service-oriented approaches.

A. Creating AI-Based Products

1. **Developing Software Applications:** The development of AI-based software applications is a potent avenue for monetization. These applications can range from specialized tools for data analysis to consumer-facing applications that leverage AI for personalized experiences. Entrepreneurs can target specific industries or user needs, creating products that offer innovative solutions and cater to a broad or niche market.

2. **Building AI-Powered Tools:** Building tools that harness the power of AI can lead to the creation of valuable assets for businesses and individuals. This could involve developing tools for data processing, automation, or even design. For instance, a tool that automates repetitive tasks using Machine Learning algorithms can find applications across various sectors, providing efficiency gains and cost savings.

B. Offering AI Services

1. **Consultation and Advisory Services:** Providing consultation and advisory services in the realm of AI is a lucrative path for individuals and firms with expertise in the field. Businesses seeking to integrate AI into their operations often require guidance on strategy, implementation, and optimization. Offering consultancy services allows experts to share their

knowledge, helping clients make informed decisions about AI adoption.

2. **Customized Solutions for Businesses:** Tailoring AI solutions to meet the specific needs of businesses is a high-demand service. This involves understanding the unique challenges faced by a client and developing customized AI applications to address those challenges. Whether it's enhancing customer experiences, optimizing supply chain processes, or improving data security, providing bespoke solutions adds significant value to clients.

C. Exploring AI in Entrepreneurship

1. **Startups and Innovation:** The startup ecosystem is rife with opportunities for entrepreneurs to innovate and disrupt industries using AI. Creating a startup that leverages AI technology allows for the development of novel solutions and services. Startups can target emerging markets or address existing challenges in unconventional ways, positioning themselves as pioneers in the AI space.

2. **Partnership Opportunities:** Collaboration and partnerships present a strategic approach to monetizing AI. Entrepreneurs can explore partnerships with existing businesses to integrate AI into their operations or products. This collaborative approach allows for shared resources, expertise, and market access. It's a mutually beneficial avenue where the entrepreneurial spirit combines with established entities to drive innovation.

Monetizing AI projects requires a strategic approach that aligns with market demands and leverages the unique strengths of AI technology. Whether through the creation of innovative products, the provision of expert services, or entrepreneurial ventures, individuals and businesses can tap into the vast potential of AI to not only drive innovation but also generate substantial revenue. In the subsequent sections, we will delve into specific strategies and considerations for successful AI monetization.

V. Chat GPT: A Specialized Section

In the realm of Artificial Intelligence, conversational AI has emerged as a transformative force, redefining how humans interact with machines. Chat GPT, a powerful language model developed by OpenAI, stands at the forefront of this revolution. This section explores the intricacies of Chat GPT, its potential applications, and how individuals and businesses can leverage it for effective monetization.

A. Introduction to Chat GPT

1. **Overview of Conversational AI:** Conversational AI involves the development of systems that enable machines to understand, interpret, and respond to human language in a natural and coherent manner. Chat GPT, short for Chat Generative Pre-trained Transformer, represents a breakthrough in this domain. It is a state-of-the-art language model designed to generate human-like text, making it well-suited for a variety of conversational applications.

2. **Potential Applications:** Chat GPT's versatility opens the door to a wide range of applications. From chatbots and virtual assistants to content generation and interactive storytelling, its capabilities extend across diverse industries. The model's ability to understand context and generate contextually relevant responses positions it as a valuable tool for enhancing user experiences in numerous contexts.

B. Leveraging Chat GPT for Monetization

1. **Content Creation and Blogging:** Chat GPT can be harnessed for content creation, generating engaging and coherent articles, blog posts, and marketing copy. Content creators and bloggers can leverage Chat GPT to enhance productivity, ideation, and creativity. By automating certain aspects of content generation,

individuals and businesses can focus on strategy and quality, while reducing the time and effort required for routine tasks.

2. **Virtual Assistance and Customer Support:** Embedding Chat GPT in virtual assistants and customer support systems elevates the quality of interactions. It enables more natural and context-aware conversations, improving user satisfaction. Businesses can deploy Chat GPT-powered virtual assistants to handle routine queries, provide information, and even assist in troubleshooting, freeing up human resources for more complex tasks.

3. **Social Media Management:** Social media platforms thrive on engaging and relevant content. Chat GPT can be employed for social media management, aiding in the generation of posts, responses, and even formulating social media strategies. Automating aspects of social media content creation allows individuals and businesses to maintain a consistent online presence and engage with their audience effectively.

C. Case Studies

1. **Success Stories of Individuals/Companies Using Chat GPT:** Examining real-world success stories provides valuable insights into the potential impact of Chat GPT. From startups streamlining customer interactions to established companies enhancing their marketing strategies, these case studies showcase the diverse ways in which Chat GPT can be applied for tangible results.

2. **Lessons Learned and Best Practices:** Analysing the experiences of those who have successfully implemented Chat GPT reveals important lessons and best practices. Understanding the challenges faced and the strategies employed by others ensures a more informed approach to implementation. Considerations

such as fine-tuning, ethical use, and ongoing monitoring are crucial for maximizing the benefits of Chat GPT.

In this specialized section, we've explored the capabilities of Chat GPT, its potential applications for monetization, and real-world examples that illuminate the possibilities and challenges. As technology continues to advance, the integration of Chat GPT into various aspects of communication and content creation holds the promise of reshaping how we interact with information and services.

VI. Legal and Ethical Considerations

As the world of AI continues to evolve and integrate into various aspects of our lives, addressing legal and ethical considerations becomes imperative. This section delves into the complex landscape of legal and ethical considerations in AI monetization, emphasizing the importance of responsible practices.

A. Intellectual Property and Data Privacy

1. **Intellectual Property:** In the realm of AI, intellectual property concerns extend to the algorithms, models, and innovations created. Individuals and businesses must carefully consider how to protect their intellectual property rights. This involves understanding patent laws, trade secrets, and licensing agreements. Striking a balance between sharing knowledge for collaboration and safeguarding proprietary technology is crucial for sustained success.

2. **Data Privacy:** The utilization of AI often involves the collection and analysis of vast amounts of data. Ensuring compliance with data privacy regulations is paramount. Individuals have the right to know how their data is being used and must provide informed consent. Implementing robust data encryption, anonymization practices, and transparent data policies is essential for maintaining trust and adhering to legal standards.

B. Ethical Considerations in AI Monetization

1. **Fair and Unbiased AI:** AI systems can inadvertently perpetuate biases present in training data. Ensuring fairness and unbiased decision-making is critical. Developers must actively work to identify and rectify bias within AI models. This involves continuous monitoring, evaluation, and refinement of algorithms to minimize discriminatory outcomes.

2. **Transparency and Explainability:** Transparent AI systems build trust with users. Understanding how AI decisions are made is crucial for users and stakeholders. Developers should prioritize creating AI models that are explainable, allowing users to comprehend the rationale behind decisions. This transparency fosters accountability and ensures ethical AI practices.

3. **Human-Centric Design:** AI systems should be designed with human well-being in mind. Ethical considerations encompass issues such as job displacement, societal impact, and unintended consequences. Developers and businesses should prioritize solutions that enhance human experiences, create positive societal impacts, and minimize adverse effects.

C. Compliance with Regulations and Standards

1. **GDPR and Data Protection Laws:** The General Data Protection Regulation (GDPR) and other data protection laws impose stringent requirements on how personal data is handled. Compliance with these regulations is non-negotiable. Businesses must understand the legal obligations related to data processing, storage, and transfer, and implement measures to meet these standards.

2. **Industry-Specific Regulations:** Different industries may have specific regulations governing the use of AI. For example, healthcare and finance have stringent regulations due to the sensitive nature of data involved. Businesses must stay abreast of industry-specific regulations and ensure their AI practices align with these standards.

3. **Ethical AI Guidelines:** Various organizations and bodies have established ethical guidelines for AI development and deployment. Adhering to principles outlined by institutions such as the IEEE, the Partnership on AI,

and national AI ethics boards is essential. Aligning with these guidelines helps ensure responsible and ethical AI practices.

In the dynamic landscape of AI monetization, legal and ethical considerations are not static; they evolve with technology and societal expectations. A commitment to responsible practices, transparent decision-making, and ongoing compliance with regulations will be instrumental in building a sustainable and ethical foundation for AI-driven ventures.

VII. Future Trends in AI Monetization

The landscape of AI monetization is continually evolving, driven by advancements in technology, changing market dynamics, and emerging trends. This section explores the future trajectories of AI monetization, shedding light on emerging technologies and predictions for the AI market.

A. Emerging Technologies in AI

1. **Generative AI Advancements:** Generative AI, particularly in the context of language models and image generation, is poised for significant advancements. Models like GPT-4, successors to Chat GPT, are anticipated to exhibit even greater language understanding and creative capabilities. This opens up new avenues for content creation, storytelling, and interactive experiences, presenting opportunities for individuals and businesses to monetize innovative applications.

2. **AI in Decentralized Finance:** The intersection of AI and decentralized finance (DeFi) is an exciting frontier. AI algorithms can be applied to analyse complex financial data, optimize trading strategies, and enhance risk management within decentralized ecosystems. Smart contracts and blockchain technologies, coupled with AI, have the potential to revolutionize financial services, creating opportunities for novel AI-driven DeFi applications and services.

B. Predictions and Forecasts for the AI Market

1. **AI Market Growth:** The AI market is poised for substantial growth in the coming years. Predictions indicate an exponential increase in the adoption of AI technologies across diverse industries, leading to a surge in market size. Businesses and entrepreneurs who strategically position themselves within this expanding

market stand to benefit from the growing demand for AI-driven solutions.

2. **Industry-Specific AI Solutions:** The future of AI monetization lies in the development of industry-specific solutions. As AI becomes more ingrained in various sectors, there will be a shift towards tailored applications that address specific challenges within healthcare, finance, manufacturing, and more. Entrepreneurs who specialize in creating targeted AI solutions for niche industries are likely to find lucrative opportunities.

3. **AI-Powered Sustainability Solutions:** With an increased emphasis on sustainability and environmental consciousness, AI is expected to play a vital role in developing innovative solutions. Predictive analytics and machine learning algorithms can be employed to optimize energy consumption, reduce waste, and enhance sustainability practices. Entrepreneurs focusing on AI-driven sustainability initiatives may find a growing market for their solutions.

4. **Integration of AI and IoT:** The integration of AI and the Internet of Things (IoT) is a trend set to reshape industries. AI algorithms can analyse vast amounts of data generated by interconnected devices, enabling more informed decision-making and automation. Entrepreneurs exploring opportunities at the intersection of AI and IoT stand to benefit from the synergies created by these two transformative technologies.

5. **AI-Driven Personalization:** Personalization powered by AI is expected to reach new heights. Businesses will increasingly leverage AI algorithms to analyse user behaviour, preferences, and historical data to deliver

hyper-personalized experiences. Entrepreneurs in e-commerce, content creation, and customer engagement can capitalize on the demand for tailored and personalized AI-driven services.

As we look toward the future, the convergence of emerging technologies and evolving market demands creates a landscape rich with opportunities for AI monetization. Entrepreneurs and businesses that stay attuned to these trends, embrace innovation, and adapt their strategies accordingly are poised to shape and benefit from the unfolding future of AI.

VIII. Conclusion

In the journey through the realms of AI and monetization, we've traversed the expansive landscape of possibilities, challenges, and future horizons. As we conclude this guide, let's reflect on key points, provide encouragement, and issue a call-to-action for those eager to embark on the transformative journey of AI monetization.

A. Recap of Key Points

1. **AI's Expansive Landscape:** The overview of AI applications, from Machine Learning to Natural Language Processing and Computer Vision, showcased the diversity and impact of AI across industries.

2. **Building AI Skills:** We explored the essential technical skills, including programming languages and data analysis, as well as crucial non-technical skills such as business acumen and problem-solving.

3. **Monetizing AI Projects:** Whether through creating AI-based products or offering services, there are various avenues for individuals and businesses to turn their AI endeavours into profitable ventures.

4. **Chat GPT Specialization:** The specialized section on Chat GPT highlighted the potential of conversational AI, particularly in content creation, virtual assistance, and social media management.

5. **Legal and Ethical Considerations:** Intellectual property, data privacy, and ethical AI practices were emphasized as critical considerations in the responsible development and deployment of AI solutions.

6. **Future Trends:** The exploration of emerging technologies like generative AI and the intersection of AI with decentralized finance, coupled with predictions for the AI market, illuminated the evolving landscape.

B. Encouragement and Motivation for Readers

As you navigate the complexities of AI monetization, remember that this journey is not solely about technology; it's about your unique perspective, innovation, and resilience. Embrace the challenges as opportunities for growth and celebrate the victories —big and small—that come with each step forward.

The world of AI is dynamic and ever evolving, offering room for both seasoned professionals and newcomers to make meaningful contributions. Your skills, ideas, and determination have the power to shape the future of AI monetization.

C. Call-to-Action for Embarking on AI Monetization Journey

Now, it's time for action. Whether you are a seasoned professional or someone just beginning to explore the possibilities of AI, take that first step. Here's your call-to-action:

1. **Deepen Your Skills:** Continuously invest in enhancing your technical and non-technical skills. Embrace lifelong learning, engage with communities, and stay abreast of the latest developments in AI.

2. **Identify Opportunities:** Explore the unique challenges within industries or sectors that align with your interests. Identify opportunities where AI can provide innovative solutions or enhancements.

3. **Network and Collaborate:** Connect with professionals, organizations, and communities in the AI space. Collaboration often leads to new perspectives, ideas, and potential partnerships that can amplify your impact.

4. **Stay Ethical and Responsible:** Uphold ethical standards in your AI endeavours. Consider the broader societal impact of your work and ensure compliance with legal and ethical guidelines.

5. **Embrace Innovation:** Be open to innovation and experimentation. The fusion of AI with emerging technologies creates fertile ground for groundbreaking

ideas. Embrace the unknown and pioneer new solutions.

Embark on your AI monetization journey with confidence, curiosity, and a commitment to creating positive impact. The future is yours to shape, and the potential within the realms of AI is vast. May your journey be filled with discovery, innovation, and the realization of your aspirations in the ever-evolving world of AI monetization.

IX. Additional Resources

As you delve deeper into the world of AI monetization, continuous learning and staying updated with the latest tools and resources are paramount. This section provides a curated list of recommended books, courses, websites, and tools that can serve as valuable companions on your journey.

A. Recommended Books, Courses, and Websites for Further Learning

1. **Books:**
   - "Artificial Intelligence: A Guide for Thinking Humans" by Melanie Mitchell
   - "Life 3.0: Being Human in the Age of Artificial Intelligence" by Max Tegmark
   - "Python Machine Learning" by Sebastian Raschka and Vahid Mirjalili
   - "AI Superpowers: China, Silicon Valley, and the New World Order" by Kai-Fu Lee

2. **Online Courses:**
   - Coursera: Machine Learning by Andrew Ng
   - edX: Artificial Intelligence (AI) by Microsoft
   - Udacity: AI for Everyone by Andrew Ng
   - Fast.ai: Practical Deep Learning for Coders

3. **Websites and Platforms:**
   - TensorFlow: An open-source machine learning framework by Google.
   - PyTorch: A popular deep learning library for research and production.
   - Kaggle: A platform for data science competitions and datasets.
   - Towards Data Science: A Medium publication

covering a wide range of AI and data science topics.

- ArXiv.org: A repository of academic papers in the fields of AI, machine learning, and more.

B. Tools and Platforms for AI Development and Deployment

1. **Development Frameworks:**
   - Jupyter Notebooks: An open-source web application that allows you to create and share documents that contain live code, equations, visualizations, and narrative text.
   - Anaconda: A distribution of Python and R for scientific computing, used for data science, machine learning, and AI.

2. **Machine Learning Platforms:**
   - Google Colab: A free, cloud-based Jupyter notebook environment that allows for easy access to GPUs for machine learning tasks.
   - Azure Machine Learning: A cloud service for building, training, and deploying machine learning models.

3. **Deployment Platforms:**
   - Heroku: A cloud platform that enables developers to deploy and scale applications effortlessly.
   - AWS SageMaker: A fully managed service that enables developers to build, train, and deploy machine learning models at scale.

4. **Version Control:**
   - Git: A distributed version control system widely used for source code management.
   - GitHub: A web-based platform for version control and collaboration using Git.

These resources serve as stepping stones, providing the knowledge and tools needed to navigate the intricate landscape of AI. Remember that learning is a continuous process, and staying curious and engaged is key to unlocking the full potential of AI monetization.

Closing Thoughts and Thank You

As we reach the final pages of this guide, I want to express my sincere appreciation for accompanying you on this journey through the vast landscapes of AI monetization. The world of artificial intelligence is dynamic, ever evolving, and filled with endless possibilities.

As you set forth on your own AI monetization journey, remember that this is not merely a technical expedition but a fusion of creativity, innovation, and ethical responsibility. Each step you take, each idea you nurture, contributes to the transformative power of AI.

In the realm of AI, challenges are opportunities, and every innovation has the potential to shape the future. Embrace the unknown, be resilient in the face of challenges, and celebrate the small victories that pave the way for greater successes.

As you navigate the complexities of AI, always keep learning, stay curious, and remain adaptable. The world of technology waits for no one, and your curiosity will be the compass that guides you through the ever-expanding frontiers of AI.

Thank you for entrusting your time and curiosity to this exploration. Whether you are a seasoned professional, an aspiring entrepreneur, or someone taking their first steps into the world of AI, your dedication to learning and growth is the catalyst for progress.

May your journey be filled with discovery, innovation, and the fulfilment of your aspirations. The future is yours to shape, and I wish you every success in your endeavours.

Thank you, and here's to the exciting and boundless possibilities that await in the world of AI.

BOOKS BY THIS AUTHOR

The Ultimate Guide To Online Marketing Mastery

From mastering SEO to leveraging social media, email marketing, and more, this guide offers a strategic approach to building a powerful online presence. Whether you're a budding entrepreneur or an established business owner, you'll find invaluable insights and practical strategies to propel your brand forward.

Never Say 'I Don't Know'

Through captivating narratives and proven strategies, this book reveals the power of curiosity, the art of strategic networking, and the limitless potential of continuous learning. It's not just a guide; it's a mentor, providing the insights and expertise you need to conquer the dynamic world of entrepreneurship.

Fortunes Unveiled: The Journeys Of The World's Top 100 Richest People

From Silicon Valley's tech giants to Wall Street's financial magnates, from self-made entrepreneurs to heirs of colossal fortunes, this book unravels the captivating narratives that have shaped the contemporary wealth landscape. Each chapter is a profound lesson in ambition, resilience, and unwavering dedication to excellence.

www.ingramcontent.com/pod-product-compliance
Lightning Source LLC
Chambersburg PA
CBHW072226290526
45794CB00007B/2913